Are Cows Afraid of Moonsters?
jokes for kids and very silly adults

V. Byrd

Copyright 2023 V. Byrd
All rights reserved.

Do cows like books?

Yes, but they are partial to mooooosteries.

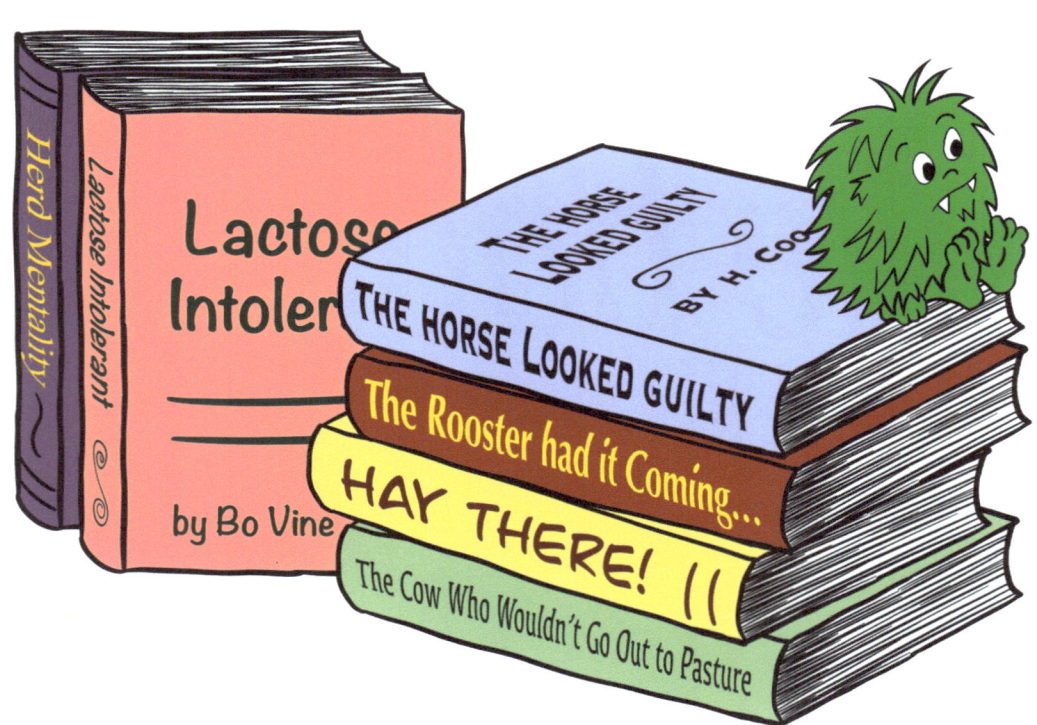

Can cows fly?

It would take a mooooracle.

Why don't cows like peas?

Because they're too mooooshy.

What did the cow want on his pizza?

Mooooozzarella!

What kind of candy do cows like?

Caramoooool.

Why did the cow go to the dentist?

He was having trouble with a mooooolar.

Why did the cow want to go to the city?

To see a moooooosical.

How did he get there?

He took a mooooober.

Where do cows go to see dinosaurs?

A moooooseum.

Why did the cow need an eraser?

Because he made a mooooostake.

Why was the cow itchy?

He had a mooooosquito bite.

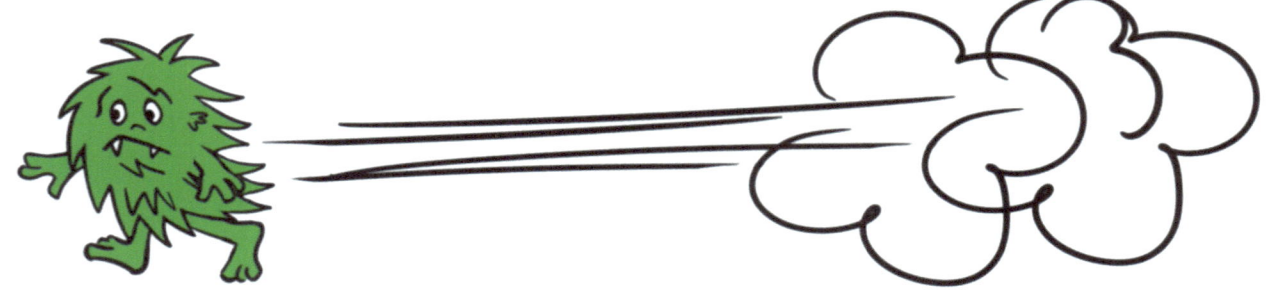

What do you call a cow that does magic tricks?

A mooooogician.

Why did the cow say, "Excuse me"?

Because he wanted you to mooooove.

Why was the cow unrecognizable?

Because he was wearing a fake mooooostache.

How do cows meet other cows?

Mooootual friends.

How much sleep do cows need?

Eight hours moooonimum.

www.ingramcontent.com/pod-product-compliance
Lightning Source LLC
Chambersburg PA
CBHW040723060526
44119CB00083B/308